HOW TO MAKE
YOGURT PARFAIT

Written by Katie Baker

Illustrated by Vanessa Cossette

How to make Yogurt Parfait
Text © 2025 Katie Baker
Illustration © 2025 Vanessa Cossette

All rights reserved.
No part of this publication may be reproduced, stored in a retrieval system, or transmitted in any form or by any means ; electronic, mechanical, photocopying, recording, or otherwise without the prior written permission of the publisher, except in the case of brief quotations used in reviews and noncommercial uses permitted by copyright law.

For permission please contact:
Katie Baker Books
KatieBakerBooks@gmail.com

www.KatieBakerBooks.com

First Edition, 2025

ISBN : 978-1-0688031-5-4

Legal Deposit – Library and Archives Canada 2025

To my kitchen explorers;
Experiment, Try new things, get messy.

There are only 3 rules:
1. Wash your hands
2. Clean up as you go
3. Be safe and have fun

In my kitchen,
It's the morning.
My tummy rumbles
Sounds like roaring.
The sun is shining,
The window's bright,
My kitten's asleep,
A cozy sight.

Let's make breakfast,
Something healthy but sweet.
Yogurt Parfait!
A morning treat.
I know what to do,
I'll start with a bowl
Ready to roll,
I'm in control.

Bananas sliced
From end to end.
Tossing the peel
Onto my friend.
Put the slices in,
Like a banana split,
Put them in first
To make sure that they fit.

In between bananas
goes the Yogurt scoops,
It falls off the spoon
In neat little bloops.
Don't add too much,
leave some space
For all of the toppings
we'll put into place.

Fresh berries,
Red and blue,
Ripe and juicy,
Ready to chew.
Layered gently,
With so much care,
Onto the yogurt,
Try one, if you dare

Homemade granola,
full of yummy things,
Mom keeps in a jar
Tied with a string.
Sprinkle, sprinkle,
Adding a crunch.
Granola's always
good to munch!

Whipped cream swirl
Err.. pile? Not bad!
Mmm... into my mouth!
Shhh... don't tell dad.
A recipe easy as,
One, two, three,
Yogurt, granola,
Bananas and cream.

Final touches,
A sprinkle more.
More Fresh berries,
That I Adore!
I made my own
Breakfast treat!
Yogurt Parfait
Ready to eat!

To the table,
Careful and steady,
Spoon in my hand,
I'm finally ready.
Proud of my work,
Feels like a thrill.
I made breakfast
An important skill!

I look at mom,
"I did it myself!"
She smiles at me,
"It's good for your health"
Laughter and smiles,
Tummy is glad,
Yogurt parfait,
"Let's make one for dad!"

Kitchen Measurements

Measurement	Metric	(U.S.)	Notes / Tip
1 pinch	1 ml	⅛ to ₁⁄₁₆ teaspoon	A tiny amount—what fits between your thumb & finger
1 teaspoon	5 ml	⅓ Tablespoon	Sometimes written as 't' or tsp
1 Tablespoon	15 ml	3 teaspoons	Often written as 'T' or Tbsp
⅛ cup	30 ml	2 Tablespoons	1 fluid ounce (fl oz)
¼ cup	60 ml	4 Tablespoons	2 fluid ounce (fl oz)
⅓ cup	80 ml	5 Tablespoons	3 fluid ounces (fl oz)
½ cup	120 ml	8 Tablespoons	4 fluid ounce (fl oz)
⅔ cup	160 ml	11 Tablespoons	5 fluid ounce (fl oz)
¾ cup	180 ml	12 Tablespoons	6 fluid ounce (fl oz)
1 cup	250 ml	16 Tablespoons	8 fluid ounce (fl oz)
1 pint (pt)	500 ml	2 cups	16 fluid ounce (fl oz)
1 quart (qt)	1000 ml	1 Litre	32 fluid ounce (fl oz)
1 gallon (gal)	3.8 liters	16 cups	4 quarts

Kitchen Symbols

° - Degrees
°C - Degrees in Celsius
°F - Degrees in Ferinheit
T - TBSP - Tablespoon - 15ml
t - tsp - Teaspoon - 5ml
ml - Mililitres
L - Litre
g - gram
kg - kilogram
c - cup
oz - ounce
lbs - pounds
hrs - hours
mins - minutes
dash/pinch- ⅛ teaspoon or less
GF - Gluten Free

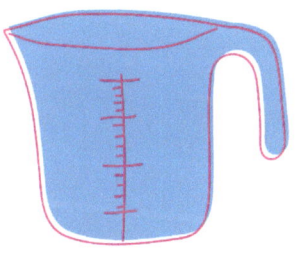
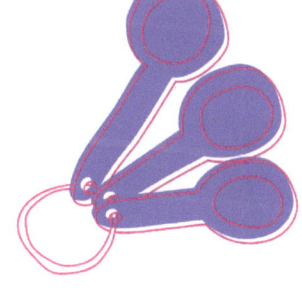

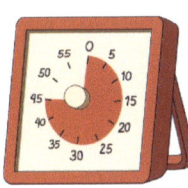

Kitchen Vocabulary

Layer – To put one thing on top of another.
Measure – To find out how much of something you need using cups or spoons.
Mix – To stir or blend things together.
Peel – To take the skin off a fruit or vegetable.
Pour – To let a liquid flow out of a cup or jug.
Scoop – To pick up food with a spoon or cup.
Slice – To cut something into flat, thin pieces.
Stir – To move a spoon round and round to blend things.
Spread – To cover something evenly, like butter on toast.
Sprinkle – To lightly drop small pieces or a little bit of something on top.
Taste – To try a little bit of food to see how it tastes.

Cook like a pro:
Saftey tips you should know

- Always wash hands before cooking
- Ask an adult before using knives, stoves, or ovens
- Ask for help when moving something that is hot or heavy
- Tie back long hair and roll up sleeves.
- Clean up spills to prevent slips
- Never touch hot pans or trays without help
- Use two hands to carry your dish to the table
- Wear an apron to protect from splashes
- Read your recipe 3 times before you start
- Gather and measure everything you will need before you start cooking or baking

Homemade Granola Recipe

3 cups Rolled Oats
¼ cup coconut oil (or butter)
⅓ cup Maple Syrup (or honey)
1 tsp Cinnamon
- Optional - 1 cup chopped nuts or dried fruit

Method
1. Preheat oven to 300 °F
2. Prepare a baking sheet with parchment if desired for easy clean up (DO NOT USE wax paper).
3. In a large bowl, combine all ingredients, Mix well
4. Spread mixture evenly onto baking sheet.
5. Bake for 25 to 30 minutes or until lightly golden brown.
6. Let it cool completely until it's crunchy
7. Break into clumps and store in a container with a tight lid for up to 2 weeks.

Yogurt Parfait Recipe

1 Banana sliced lengthways
½ cup Yogurt (flavour of your choice)
¼ cup Granola (home made or store bought)
¼ cup Berries (or chopped fruit of your choice)
Whipped cream

Method
1. Lay each half of the banana on either side of your bowl or dish
2. Place the yogurt between the banana slices
3. Sprinkle granola on top of the yogurt
4. Sprinkle berries on top of granola
5. Place your whipped cream on top of the berries
6. Enjoy!

www.ingramcontent.com/pod-product-compliance
Lightning Source LLC
Chambersburg PA
CBHW041121070526
44584CB00002B/232